What S

I Wear?

Written by Penny Lee

On a sunny day

I wear my T-shirt.

On a cloudy day

I wear my T-shirt

and my jumper.

On a rainy day

I wear my T-shirt

and my jumper

and my coat.

On a windy day

I wear my T-shirt

and my jumper

and my coat

and my scarf.

On a snowy day

I wear my T-shirt

and my jumper

and my coat

and my scarf

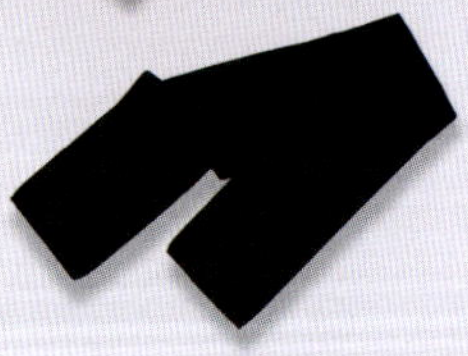

and my gloves.

Sunny

Cloudy

Rainy

Windy

Snowy